Conscious Dying

Reverend Davida Laura Preves

PublishAmerica
Baltimore

© 2010 by Reverend Davida Laura Preves.
All rights reserved. No part of this book may be reproduced, stored in a retrieval system or transmitted in any form or by any means without the prior written permission of the publishers, except by a reviewer who may quote brief passages in a review to be printed in a newspaper, magazine or journal.

First printing

PublishAmerica has allowed this work to remain exactly as the author intended, verbatim, without editorial input.

Hardcover 978-1-4489-3739-4
Softcover 978-1-4489-4782-9
PUBLISHED BY PUBLISHAMERICA, LLLP
www.publishamerica.com
Baltimore

Printed in the United States of America

To:
Sharon Elaine Preves
Scott Helgeson
Cori Ofstead
Judy Preves Anderson
Lonnie Helgeson
Laurel Ely
Carol Moen
who walked along my side during the death process. You are angels on earth.

Table of Contents

Chapter 1: Coolness of Death 9
Chapter 2: Diagnosis 11
Chapter 3: Celebration 14
Chapter 4: Following Your Intuition 16
Chapter 5: Stroke 18
Chapter 6: Dying 19
Chapter 7: Hannah: A Special Bond 24
Chapter 8: The Beauty of Death 26
Chapter 9: Halloween 28
Chapter 10: Death Date 31
Chapter 11: Musical Mattresses 33
Chapter 12: Our Changing Family 35
Chapter 13: Inner Strength 37
Chapter 14: Mom's Final Letter 40
Chapter 15: My Birthday 43
Chapter 16: Active Dying 59
Chapter 17: Mom's Death 65
Chapter 18: A Visit from Mom 70
Chapter 19: Memorial Service 73
Chapter 20: Friends 82
Chapter 21: A "First" Without Mom 86
Chapter 22: Probate Court 89
Chapter 23: Selling Mom's House 91

Chapter 24: The Piano 93
Chapter 25: One Year Post Diagnosis 97
Chapter 26: Remembrance Ceremony 101
Afterword 105

Obituary Notice:
Saint Paul Pioneer Press, November 17, 2006

SPCO violist Alice Preves dies
BY DOMINIC P. PAPATOLA
Pioneer Press

Alice Preves played viola with the St. Paul Chamber Orchestra for almost four decades, but she had the unusual distinction of earning her position within the ensemble three separate times.

Preves, who died Wednesday at 65 from complications of liver cancer, first started playing with the orchestra in the 1960s under music director Leopold Sipe. She stepped down twice after giving birth to her daughters, Laura and Sharon. She auditioned and won her chair back each time under conductors Dennis Russell Davies and Pinchas Zukerman.

Preves played consistently with the SPCO from 1982 until her retirement this fall.

"She chose to live her life in joy," said daughter Davida Laura Preves." She did that. And she truly loved her job at the chamber orchestra. She always said, 'I get to go to work,' instead of 'I have to go to work.' "

Tamas Strasser, who sat next to Preves in the orchestra for more than two decades, said Preves' interests ventured far beyond classical music. She was a student of Judaism and alternative healing; her background as a music teacher and her listening skills naturally led her, in later years, to become certified as a life coach.

"A stand partner is a very important person in your life; you spend more time with them than you do your spouse," Strasser said. "And you never know who you're going to get. I was very fortunate to get Alice. She was forthright, and she was conscientious, and we trusted each other. We used to complete each other's sentences."

Preves was diagnosed with liver cancer in August and retired from the orchestra the following month. In the months before her death, Preves made a contribution to the orchestra to endow her seat, helping to support the position in the orchestra in perpetuity. Her replacement will sit in the Alice Preves Viola Chair.

Chapter 1
Coolness of Death

Wednesday, November 15, 2006

Mom died today at 3:40 p.m.

As my sister and I held Mom's body, the temperature of her skin seemed to change and became very cool. Much to our relief, the room felt so peaceful.

It was very important to Sharon to be alone with Mom's body. We are so very different. I didn't really feel any attachment to Mom's body. It just seemed like it was broken vehicle, and needed to be traded in for something better.

When I was sitting in the living room with family members, I felt the whole aura of the house change…a coolness, like fresh cleansing air, was being swept throughout the house. My husband Scott had gone to get the kids at school. When Scott called me at about 3:55 p.m., I told him, "Mom has died. How should we handle this with the kids? Am I supposed to tell them in person or have you and (Scott's brother) Stefan do it?"

This all seemed overwhelming to me. Looking back, it probably doesn't matter who is there. They just need to be told gently and with love.

My husband told the girls together at our house, and then he brought two of the girls to Mom's house because they wanted to see her body before it was taken away.

My sister Sharon, sister-in-law Lonnie, and our home health aid Margaret did a wonderful job of cleaning Mom's body and dressing her in a beautiful lacy, ivory satin robe. She looked so peaceful—much more peaceful than she had looked for so many days. Her mouth wouldn't stay closed so we rolled up a towel under her chin. It worked—so that when the kids arrived, her mouth was mostly closed.

Sharon lit candles in the room and started playing Uncle Jeffery's "Keyboard Conversations" CDs. The room felt nice, peaceful, pleasant—for the first time in so many days and weeks. Jeffrey Siegel was a dear friend of Mom's, and my god father, but he is also a world-renowned pianist and famous among music circles for his "Keyboard Conversations."

Everyone sat together in Mom's living room—drained, relieved, sad—so deeply sad.

Chapter 2
Diagnosis

July 27, 2006

Mom and Sharon just called on their way back from their biannual pilgrimage to Rochester's Mayo Clinic to see the doctor. Despite the circumstances and the inconvenience of an exam here or there, Sharon and Mom looked forward to these visits and considered these trips mini-getaways. They'd been doing this for five years—ever since Mom's diagnosis of "end stage" primary biliary cirrhosis—an autoimmune disease of the bile ducts. My sister loved the medical jargon and helped Mom interpret what was being said in the meetings with the doctor.

As customary, they always called me while driving home from Rochester. When Mom said the dreaded words "liver cancer," I had to sit down. After working briefly at the American Liver Foundation, I knew that liver cancer was not a promising diagnosis. It seemed a certain death sentence.

Mom (always the optimist) assured me that this was simply a blood test gone bad, and that her doctor wanted her back in for tests in a day or two.

Finally, it was my turn to have the Rochester experience as I made the pilgrimage this time. What an amazing little city Rochester is, like an unknown world dropped into the middle of the country. This is a place where miracles happen. So much care has been taken in setting up the Mayo Clinic, filling it with beautiful artwork, comfortable furniture, museums, and shops. People from all over the world were dragging themselves about in the 100-degree heat.

Mom had more tests with not-good news, but still not a definite prognosis. Sharon drove down for the final test: an MRI.

August 1

Mother and daughters huddled together in the doctor's office for the results. Dr. P is a beautiful, tall man full of kindness and gentleness. As he entered, we could tell that things were not good. Mom definitely had hepatocellular carcinoma, and it had spread into the portal vein, erasing her chance for a transplant. The doctor said that her prognosis was grim—and she needed to get her affairs in order.

At that moment, I felt more devastated for Dr. P than for Mom, Sharon or me. He seemed so vulnerable and in such great despair. It must be so difficult to deliver this news as a part of his job.

Heavy laden with the news, we went to lunch at Mom's favorite place: Victoria's. She began outlining her memorial service immediately, picking the songs to be performed at the service and who would participate. This all seemed so surreal.

*How could this be happening to my mom?
She is the amazing Alice, the leader of everything,
and the woman who shows me the way.*

The Early Days After Aiagnosis

Days after coming home from Mayo Clinic, Mom and I were sitting on my deck enjoying the beautiful summer day. She began to cry and said that she didn't want to go because she knew that I still needed her. I hugged her and said that she was right, I did still need her, but I knew that I'd be alright, and that I could handle the raising of my family without her. For some reason, this moment sticks out as being particularly poignant—something about the willingness to admit my vulnerability—and to show her my strength at the same time.

I grieved and grieved during these early weeks. I've never felt so tired in my life, like I'd been run over by something. Literally I had trouble moving my body from one spot to the next. I was so grateful when school started, and also grateful that this feeling had dissipated, even now, before Mom's death. I know that it will probably come again, but this is a much-appreciated brief respite.

Chapter 3
Celebration

One of Sharon's colleagues mentioned that our family might find great help in communicating with the thousands of Mom's admirer's by using a website called Caring Bridge. Sharon went about setting up the site, and it immediately proved invaluable in managing the hundreds of calls and letters that were starting to pour in. We just sent out a mass e-mail to everyone that Mom knows to tell them that we will be posting regular news on Caring Bridge. Caring Bridge is interactive too, so we can receive all kinds of well wishes from friends and family all over the world.

Caring Bridge Entry
SUNDAY, SEPTEMBER 10, 2006 02:21 PM, CDT

Last night the Saint Paul Chamber Orchestra honored Alice in a moving tribute that included beautiful words from her stand partner, section leader, board chair, and orchestra president. There were several standing ovations in Alice's honor, including the entire house standing for her at the Ordway when she received flowers onstage. The Orchestra celebrated Alice with an ornate plaque that summarized her many contributions to the organization, a horse-drawn carriage ride around Rice Park in downtown Saint Paul, and flowers presented onstage by her dear stand partner Tamas Strasser. It was a wonderful evening.

Chapter 4
Following Your Intuition

Immediately after Mom's diagnosis, I weighed the idea of whether I should share her prognosis with the kids so they would hear the news from their parents, and not someone else. I felt this was very important in establishing and maintaining trust and open communication in our family. When I shared my thoughts with Mom, she was hesitant, but agreed that she wanted the kids to hear it from us.

The night I arrived home from Mayo we gathered around the dinner table. I told the kids I had to stay at Mayo for two nights because Mimi has liver cancer. Kids are so perceptive. Hannah immediately asked what kind of cancer is the worst kind. This question stunned me, and it took me a moment to respond. When I don't know what to do, I always ask for God's help. The help arrived quickly and I answered, "No kind of cancer is good to have."

For several weeks, that's all we told the kids. This intuition became an important part of the process in helping Mom to die. It was extraordinarily important around the time of Mom's September 23 stroke.

September 22

The day before her stroke, I took Mom to Regions Hospital for her regularly scheduled endoscopy to check the status of the varisces in her belly and esophagus. It was during this appointment that I started reading "The Dying Time." An overwhelming urgency came over me: Tell the kids that Mimi might die soon. That night, as we gathered for dinner, I shared that because there was no cure for their grandmother Mimi's cancer, it was very likely that she would die before Christmas. Nine-year-old Hannah let out a sob and said, "She's been like a second mother to me." Fifteen-year-old Mariah began to cry as we tried to console the girls. It was a heart-wrenching moment, but an incredibly important and well-timed moment nonetheless.

The next night, the girls witnessed Mimi's stroke and her being whisked off to the hospital by ambulance. In liver cancer, having a stroke is not common, so we had no idea this would happen.

It was the communication with the kids that allowed them to better process what happened the night Mom had the stroke. Following my intuition, when I felt an overwhelming urge to communicate with the kids about Mimi's impending death, I did, and felt so grateful that I followed this inner knowing.

When a dear friend asked Hannah how her grandmother was doing, Hannah responded, "She is nearing the end of her life." How eloquent for a little girl, and how accepting and lovely.

Chapter 5
Stroke

Caring Bridge Entry
FRIDAY, SEPTEMBER 29, 2006 03:23 PM, CDT

Hello Dear Friends,
Alice continues to rest comfortably at home with in-home hospice care and 24-hour live-in home health assistance.

Please know that although she continues to spend much of her time sleeping, she is in no pain and is quite comfortable and able to communicate well. Indeed, she is still telling jokes and being her amazingly positive self.

We share your wonderful guest book entries with her daily. This is the best way to communicate with her now. Your words bring her great joy and peace.

We will let you know if and when she wants visitors or callers.

Our love to you,
Laura and Sharon

Chapter 6
Dying

All during early October I was so fixated on the time line. That feeling began to dissipate by the third week of the month, melting into what I'd say was a profound acceptance. I watched in gratitude as my sister, my husband and our children all relaxed into this grace of acceptance. What a beautiful gift to give ourselves and each other.

At times, people would talk with me about Mom's impending death and tell me about this or that miracle—a person they knew or had heard of who defied all odds and is still living 20 years later. Every time I heard one of these stories I felt very detached from them. Actually, at first I was mad at that person. Didn't they understand that I couldn't be in the place of hope for Mom's survival? In order for my own survival and sanity, I had to accept what seemed to be inevitable.

Eventually I relaxed my anger and gave each of these people "the gift of holding that hope" for me—that I couldn't be in that place, but I appreciated that they could be for me. I realized that I had to be very gentle with myself, and those around me. Part of that was accepting my own process—and that of others.

October 24

One myth I had about hospice was that once Mom was in hospice, she wouldn't go out of the house. I was so surprised when Leslie, our wonderful nurse, ordered a wheelchair and remarked on how important it was for Mom to be able to get out and about.

Once Mom healed enough from the stroke, she attended church, lunched with friends and attended a concert or two. It was a big highlight for everyone when she even attended her music student's kung fu competition. What became clear is that even through the dying process, Mom could live a full and rich life.

This past week it has become obvious that those going-out-of-the-house days are quickly fading. Mom spends most of her time in bed and loves to be read to. She lost her ability to read a couple of weeks ago, now reading only a sentence or two before it becomes just too taxing and the meaning gets lost. My sister and I have been reading two wonderful books to her: "The Dying Time" and "The Final Gift." She loves to hear about other people's experiences as they move through their final moments of life. She listens, eyes closed, with a smile on her face. It truly is a gift to all of us to be able to share some of these most intimate and meaningful moments of our lives. The books bring about deep and thoughtful conversations. We often stop in the middle of a story or chapter to talk about Mom's own experience. Like, is she waiting for any certain event before she can die? Does she need to see her brother or not? She says no, but she wants a letter written to him. She keeps insisting that she get to November 11, and she wants to see the play "The Full Monty" at the Bloomington Art Center. Neither Sharon nor I can figure this out. Does she want to get through my birthday on November 10? We've also talked about the hidden or deeper meaning behind the title "The Full Monty"—something about having done it all, or going back to nakedness.

One of the dearest moments throughout the dying process was with Mom, our oldest daughter, 15-year-old Mariah, and me sitting around her bed. This is one of the first times we began reading "The Dying Time" to her. I was reading from the chapter about what to expect physically when you enter the dying process. The book was describing that swallowing might become very difficult and that the dying one may lose control over bodily functions. We also read about the grief over the loss of a future. This conversation touched Mariah, who tends to be a workaholic, in a deep and meaningful way. She cleared her schedule of extra events at school for an entire week, and mentioned that the meeting with Mimi made her realize that she didn't have her priorities in the proper place.

Hospice Care

What a wonderful experience hospice care has been. Now, experiencing it first hand, I have nothing but positive things to say. I have heard many people say that their loved ones were only in hospice care for a few days or a week or two. We learned that anyone with a terminal diagnosis can enroll in hospice. Mom has enjoyed the nurse visits, free medications, massage therapist, social worker and bereavement counselor.

In fact, our whole family has access to Wendy, the bereavement counselor. She has been so helpful in bringing this all into focus and holding the space for us as we do our crying. She's told me that we can continue to use her services up to 13 months after Mom's death. I know that we will take advantage of this. Her expertise with the kids is wonderful. Each of our girls has met with her. Amazingly, even our youngest, 6-year-old Faith, opened up to her, saying that she was scared of the word "death" and of cemeteries because she's afraid she's going to die.

Faith has gotten much more comfortable with the idea of dying. When she didn't want to go to Mimi's the other day, I told her we would all be happy after Mimi's death that we had spent time with her. She then asked me when Mimi is going to die. I said that only God knows. She responded, "Mimi does too."

October 29

The last few days have been hard. A few nights ago Mom had a harrowing evening—feeling like she couldn't breathe and that her heart was racing. After talking with the nurse, we decided that a lot of her discomfort was from ascitis (a collection of fluid in the belly that is common with liver failure). Mom went to have her belly tapped on Friday, to drain quite a bit of fluid. Instead, they were only able to drain less than a third of a liter and found that the entire distention of her belly is tumor—all the way from under her breastbone to her pelvic bone.

A new low. This news was very difficult, and I've been having trouble processing my emotions—feeling very tense and having difficulty breathing.

When I visited Mom yesterday, she had a savage bright-orange tan because her liver was failing and she was severely jaundiced. In my shock, it was a bit difficult to regulate my response to seeing her. Her good friend Laurel came by and was devastatingly shocked at Mom's appearance and temperament. Her face seems to be losing any affect and looked like a blank slate. I ended up consoling Laurel. This seems so backwards, and I feel so numb.

I lay awake at night exhausted and tense, both at the same time. Despite all of my attempts at self-care, nothing seems to be keeping up with my tension. I walk almost daily, do yoga several times a week, and have regular acupuncture and chiropractic treatments. Imagine the mess I'd be if I weren't doing these things.

Chapter 7
Hannah: A Special Bond

Mom and 9-year-old Hannah have always had the most special bond. I've often thought that Mom's death will be hardest on Hannah. Today, Mom seemed tired and scared, but asked to talk privately with Hannah. We have been so open with the kids throughout this process. I think the benefits of talking with the kids about death are beyond measure.

October 26

The talk with Hannah went very well. Mom seems relieved that she was able to share openly with Hannah about her own impending death. Apparently they both laughed and cried—such a gift. Mom asked Hannah if it would be okay if she would visit her from the other side. Hannah said, "That would be great." They have such a lovely relationship. I feel so sad for Hannah that she won't have Mimi to hug and love her up.

Mom told Hannah the story of Bill Ely, a dear friend who died without explanation in his sleep at age 40. The first two nights after his death, Bill came to her at night while she lay awake, asking her to "let them know I'm all right." He kept repeating it over and over until on the second night Mom agreed to let them know. Upon telling Bill's wife Laurel this story, she remarked, well, of course Bill came to you, you're the only person he knew who went to "spook school." This was referring to Mom's long-time association with the Spiritual Frontiers Fellowship and International Institute of Integral Human Sciences.

When Mom first found out she had a two-to-six-month prognosis, she went to great effort to find a surrogate grandmother for our three daughters. I don't know that anyone could ever take her place. Mom has an especially deep understanding of her important role in Hannah's life.

Chapter 8
The Beauty of Death

What has become clear to me is that death is part of life. To be talked about, planned for, celebrated, embraced, enjoyed and nurtured. Just like any other part of life. This is a sacred time—a time of grace and beauty.

Leslie, the hospice nurse, addressed Mom's concern about losing control of bodily functions. Leslie had such a lovely comment about death. She said that death is very much the same as birth. You come into this life without control of your bodily functions and you leave this life, oftentimes, in the same way.

Sharon and I spend hours each day processing this dying experience we are sharing. After leaving Mom's house, we hop on the phone with each other and talk and talk, trying to make sense of everything we are experiencing. I am so grateful to have a sister, and marvel at how she's handling this with such grace and integrity. Again I am learning from Sharon. She is so capable and able to hold the space to be present for Mom, and does this in a very different way from me. At times throughout this process, I've felt I haven't been able to do that enough. It has become obvious to me that I am doing that—in my own and unique way. And I know that Mom deeply appreciates both our approaches.

Scott and Me

I was scared that Mom's absence would put an unusually difficult burden on me with raising our three children. She has been a vital and integral part of our family and instrumental with each of the kids and their daily care. I couldn't imagine what life without her would mean or look like on a daily basis. After her stroke, this image suddenly became very clear. What arose astounds and amazes me. My husband and I are much closer as a result of having to work together more. We are functioning more as a partnership and are thriving despite this sad time. I have more respect for him than ever.

The loss of my Mom has always scared me beyond belief. Now that I'm staring it in the face, my fear is easing. My life will go on—and I will thrive. She certainly taught us how to live, and now her final gift is teaching us how to die.

Chapter 9
Halloween

Sharon called me today and told me about the incredible day she had with Mom yesterday. Again, Mom wanted to be read to from "Final Gifts." Sharon read a chapter regarding mending broken relationships at the end of life. Mom was crying, and without much warning, announced that she was ready to call her brother. Mom and her brother have not spoken to each other in years because of some sort of rift that seems very hidden, and the reason not obvious to us.

Sharon was instructed to get his number and Mom immediately called him. After many years of silence, she announced within the first minute that she was dying and had about two or three weeks to live. My uncle had trouble breathing while hearing this news in this brief conversation. When they hung up, Mom said that now that she was done with that, she only had one more thing to do before she dies. That is to see the Bloomington Civic Theater production of "The Full Monty" on November 11—almost two weeks from now! Why "The Full Monty" is so important to her we don't know, but she's been talking about it for weeks. This is a woman who has performed with the greatest musicians of our time all around the world. Why would the Bloomington Civic Theater's production be so important to her?

October 31, 2006

We celebrated Halloween today. I had two princesses in my house. Faith was a Rose Fairy and Hannah was a medieval princess. Before we hit the streets, we headed over to Mom's for our first Halloween candy. Sharon had gone out to get some candy for Mom so that she could have some to give the girls when we stopped by.

Faith was extremely resistant to going to Mimi's for our first Halloween stop. She has been so scared of death, asking me to never say the word "die" or talk about cemeteries, or anyone dying. I told her that we would be so glad that we spent time with Mimi later, when she's no longer able to be with us. Faith acquiesced and we made the 10-block trip to Mimi's house.

After all of that resistance, Faith was absolutely darling with Mom. The sweetest thing about today was when Faith sprinkled her coveted fairy dust on Mimi. Faith won't share this fairy dust with anyone. She keeps it in a small glass stopper that hangs on the end of a necklace. Always close to her and well protected.

She moved in close to Mimi's hospital bed and carefully removed the cork of her fairy dust bottle. She poured out a little of the sparkly, fine sand, and ever so gently caressed a bit on to Mimi's arm. It was so sweet, gentle and loving.

Mom has always gone trick or treating with us. This is the first year without her. Sharon came over and went around the circle with us. It felt so amazing to have her along. It would have felt so empty and sad if she had not joined us. I'm so grateful for her presence.

Chapter 10
Death Date

November 2, 2006

Sharon discussed the obit with Mom yesterday. I love how Sharon just gets it all done and discusses everything right up front. When asked if she'd like to help write her obit, Mom said no, that we should write it and then read it to her. Sharon and Mom also went through Mom's photos and selected a good photo to accompany the obit. Mom wants to use her most recent photo holding her viola. She wanted to look like herself, close to the age she actually is, instead of younger photos of her.

When going through the photos, they came across several pictures of Hannah, and Mom cried. It is so sad that Hannah is losing her best friend—she and Mom have this amazing connection. Sometimes I feel so ill equipped to help Hannah deal with this loss. I think we just need to guide her as beautifully and lovingly as Mom has all of these years.

What a great loss—that relationship between Hannah and Mom. They have been the dearest of friends for Hannah's whole life. I'm sure Hannah will use this loss in her teachings and incorporate it into her wisdom as she gets older. Mariah, Hannah and Faith are all such wise and lovely human beings. Each one of the girls has a wonderful gift to offer the world.

Tam, Mom's friend of 23 years from the orchestra, stopped by today. It was a great visit and Mom got very emotional when she said good-bye to Tam. She said she only had a couple of weeks to live and that she was "tired of being tired."

My sister and Mom had a great connection after Tam's departure. They talked about my birthday on November 10 and that her own departure date would be on the 12th. She's said this a couple of times now, once to her caregiver, Janet, and once to Sharon.

It is both comforting and strange to think that she would have that kind of control over her death. Comforting in that we all have the power to choose one of the most important dates of our lives, and strange because it seems like such a mystery. I've always thought that we have an agreement with God prior to our birth. We are guaranteed our set number of days in this life and that no matter what we do, when our time is up, our time is up.

I'll have to think about this theory more as we move through this process.

Chapter 11
Musical Mattresses

November 3, 2006

I've been reading this journal to Mom as she lies in bed and listens. She seems to enjoy my sharing my journal since she is the inspiration behind it. She just said the funniest thing" "You write with so much feeling, I feel as though I was there."

I said, "You are there Mom," and stopped immediately to write this down.

Mom has taken a turn for the worse today, and I can see it in her skin. Her spirit is still so soft and graceful, but she just seems resigned to her fate in a lovely and accepting way.

A couple of days ago Mom requested a longer bed. A medical supply company delivered the longer hospital bed, but the mattress was very hard and uncomfortable, making matters worse for Mom.

As a remedy, hospice brought some sort of a blow-up thing that was loud and never worked. It was an utter failure and extremely difficult on her because she had to spend time out of bed. We learned that the blow up thing was a necessary intermediate step in getting what is called a "Sten-barr" mattress—the Cadillac of all mattresses! I guess if you're in bed all of the time, these matters become incredibly important. Because of bureaucracy, the Sten-barr is not covered by Medicare until you have first tried the blow-up thing. Mom did her time and got a Sten-barr today!! When she lay down she said, "Oh this is marvelous—I might just stick around for this."

We both laughed. She is so amazing! She still has her sense of humor through everything!

Planning for the Memorial Service

When Tam stopped by yesterday, we asked him if he would play in a string quartet for Mom's memorial service. Of course he was honored to do so. He asked what she'd like to have played. She said the slow movement from the "American Quartet" by Dvorak. Tam said, "Oh, you're going to have me playing the boring viola part in that." Mom said, "Yes, but with a lot of feeling." We all laughed. It is so great to see her joking and having fun even in her last days!

Chapter 12
Our Changing Family

November 4, 2006

I lay awake last night thinking about the program for Mom's memorial service, planning the order of things and what pictures we'll use in the printed program. I feel haunted at night, exhausted and unable to sleep.

I know that all of this tension will dissipate after we go through this process. Sharon called me early this morning. She said she considered calling me at 1 a.m. because she also had a haunted night. I think we're both a little anxious about bringing Mom's cats, Nigel and Oliver, to their new home today. It is a huge symbol of the end. I'm relieved for the cats. Nigel has been going crazy lately, meowing constantly and following us around, staying right next to our feet. He obviously knows something is going on. I think he will relax once he's in his new home for a few days.

I made Scott go find his nice suit this morning. I wanted to know that it was at hand and in good shape so that we don't have to try to find it the day before the memorial service. Why am I doing these things? It seems a little crazy since Mom's still alive in her comfortable Stenn-bar bed.

Our Family Is Growing Smaller

Right after Mom's stroke Sharon and I both had the disturbing thought that our immediate family seems so small. It is just us, Mom and our husbands and children. With Mom's absence, it seems so incredibly small—almost scary. I am most grateful for my husband's family, too.

Mom's impending death makes me realize how important our marriage is, and how much I depend on Scott. He is really there for me and I appreciate that deeply.

The Stenn-bar bed has fallen short. Mom now says that she wants her original hospital bed back. It seems like she's just so uncomfortable in her body that any bed will feel bad. I feel a little crazy trying to make all of this work for her. I arranged through hospice to have the original mattress back, this time a longer frame to accommodate her six-foot stature.

Chapter 13
Inner Strength

November 5 and 6, 2006

Mom fell this morning, losing her balance when trying to get out of bed. I guess this is to be expected at this point because she is so very weak.

Mom's Cats—Nigel and Oliver

We brought the boys to their new home yesterday. Rick and Brad are the proud new kitty owners, and welcomed the cats so beautifully.

Once inside Rick and Brad's house, Nigel and Oliver crept out of their cages and inspected the home gingerly. Oliver immediately went inside the front hall closet and came out with dust on his whiskers. It was such an adorable sight. Within 10 minutes they were relaxed and asking to be petted. Sharon and I both feel relieved and incredibly happy for the cats.

November 6

It was ominous yesterday when Mom gave me my birthday present five days early. She has never done this before. Later in the day Sharon was talking to her. She said she gave me my present early so I'd have time to go shopping with the gift certificate and buy something to wear to her memorial service. She said she wasn't sure if I'd have time to buy something if I didn't receive the present early.

Mom also said that maybe she'd do like the aboriginal tribal people do: Sit down and ask to be taken. I hope it is that easy for her.

The Half Monty

Well, we fulfilled Mom's final wish yesterday. She was able to attend the Bloomington Civic Theatre production of "The Full Monty." We were amazed that she was able to go at all. She stayed for the first half and left due to exhaustion. The rest of us all stayed for the "full monty." It was so great and healing for the spirit to laugh out loud!!

After the play, Mom said that she had done everything she wanted to do and was ready to go. When she said good-bye, something was definitely going on. It seemed so poignant and strange all at once. She said she was so glad that her family members were in each other's hearts.

My Inner Strength

You can only create something out of something you have. I have discovered through this process of helping Mom to die that I have the ability to move through difficult times with grace and dignity. Our entire family has that ability as well. What a powerful thing to discover about myself.

I've also discovered that I am emotionally strong beyond my wildest imagination. Her absence from our family and her impending death are not crippling me as I had imagined. Instead, they are strengthening me and my family.

I've been given the opportunity to lead the way in showing others how to facilitate a beautiful and dignified death. Mom has given me that gift.

I do get tired, and need a day off every once in a while; however, for the most part, I've been strengthened and enriched.

Chapter 14
Mom's Final Letter

November 7

I just found out that Mom pretends she's too tired to open her eyes when Dan, the nurse, comes for a visit. Before finding this out, Dan said that she has taken a big downward slide with her exhaustion. Little did he know that she was just playing a game with him in order to speed up his visit.

I think this is hilarious. She is manipulating her situation to her benefit in whatever way possible. Isn't that great!!

We are sitting here watching "All My Children" together. This is a great family legacy as all of the Preves girls have watched AMC for years. Mom just reminded me that when I was in high school, I wouldn't talk to her until the show went to commercial. Standing and waiting to talk to me is how she got hooked on AMC—and still watches it. It is all my fault, you see.

Beds

The new old bed arrived yesterday. Four beds in five days!! That is a record! The most important thing is that mom thinks this one is comfortable. She has the long frame to suit her height and the short mattress. We stuffed a comforter in the end between the mattress and the bed frame to keep the mattress from scooting down and to accommodate her lovely feet.

Laughing

We have been doing a lot of laughing lately. It seems that Mom's humor is in very good shape despite her body giving out.

Sharon just arrived with today's Caring Bridge entries and reads these aloud to Mom. She is reading a particularly dramatic entry from Mom's old friend. Mom is doing an interpretive dance with her arms while laying in bed listening to this message. She is in rare form. There is nothing like watching someone who is dying doing an interpretive dance while half asleep.

November 8, 2006

Last June Mom went to see a famous healer in Brazil known as John of God. She went to see if her primary biliary cirrhosis could be cured or helped in some way. Obviously it was not. The group that traveled to Brazil from the Twin Cities is scheduled to present their findings from the trip to a church on November 19. Mom wants her own findings to be included. Here is what she dictated to me yesterday, to be read aloud on November 19 at the gathering.

> *Hello dear friends,*
> *I don't know if this comes to you before or after my death, but I can't be there myself. So,*

I'd like to say the trip to Brazil was beautiful, peaceful, colorful, and I met many new friends there. I was there because I had had primary biliary cirrhosis for five years and had been on the transplant list for a new liver. I was hoping for a miracle. The night following surgery I had terrible nightmares, which told me that I had more forgiveness to do. When I went before John of God to ask if I was complete, his message was to take 45 days of healing before having any medical tests. So, I came home, called Mayo Clinic and made my next appointment for five weeks after it was originally scheduled. I don't know if that time period was crucial in my condition or not. However, I do know that when I went to Mayo, July 27, I was told I had liver cancer, which had just begun to metastasize.

I can't help but wonder if the waiting time was fatal for me. Had I caught the cancer before it metastasized, I would have been at the top of the transplant list and given a transplant. Within the next month the tumors grew a great deal and as of this date (Nov. 7, 2006) completely fill my body. We will never know the answer. But I say don't listen to John of God, instead listen to your own body.

(As dictated by Alice Preves on Tuesday, November 7, 2006.)

Chapter 15
My Birthday

November 9, 2006

It is the day before my birthday. I think she's actually going to make it past my birthday. I've had many emotions around this. The possibility of her dying on my birthday was weighing heavy on me a few weeks ago. As time goes by I am increasingly accepting of what will or will not happen. My sister helped me put this into perspective. If Mom does die on my birthday, I can look at it as a very special date that we share—instead of a burden or with resentment. Isn't everything about perspective anyway?

Dying is like moving—your friends and family grieve your absence. You are going to a different place. Maybe you'll be able to come back for a visit. Surely we'll visit you in time.

Mom and I sat together listening to a CD of Uncle Jeffrey today. He sounded so fabulous. Eloquent in both speech and music. Mom seems so peaceful and so, so tired. She was eating Swiss cheese with her eyes closed and chewing while yawning and trying desperately not to fall asleep.

Loss of Control of the body

Sharon called me last night after she and Mom had a good discussion about Mom taking care of herself. She's getting to the point where she needs to consider a catheter—not an attractive topic to her. It must be incredibly difficult to face this decision, giving up the independence you've had your entire life. My sister and I are definitely encouraging her to move toward getting some assistance but one thing we both know for sure, this is Mom's decision, not ours.

Mom was willing to take this step of information gathering. Will she be bed bound? Will it get infected? How does all of this work? When I told Mom that Dan was stopping by later today to talk about a catheter, she showed visible distaste for that idea. It is one of the few animated emotions I've seen from her today as she is almost emotionless now.

Because she was so visibly upset by the idea of talking about the catheter, I made the mistake of mentioning that he is also stopping by to talk about a patch behind her ear to help her deal with nausea. She said, "I don't experience nausea." Of course, we've been hearing about nausea on and off for the last couple of weeks.

November 10

It's 8:45 a.m. Mom just called me and sang me happy birthday! This has been a long tradition with us. I know it took all she could muster to just croak out the first phrase. She never sounded more beautiful. And it has never meant more to me to hear my Mom sing happy birthday. It is a gift I will treasure forever.

I just met with Dan at Mom's house. Everything seemed so ominous. The first thing Dan did was grab my hand and tell me that he said good-bye to Mom. I guess I was a little shocked to hear this. He said that her heart rate is elevated and other changes to her skin indicate that death is imminent. I asked him if he meant a week or two. He said, "No, I think we're looking at days."

When I walked into Mom's room to say hello, she was crying and holding her arms out to me. I asked her if she was crying because it was my birthday. She said yes. She looked so deeply into my eyes and held my hands tight.

It is so hard for me to take what Dan says about her prognosis seriously. She was conversing with me. Asking me to clear out her dresser drawers. She seems very urgent about this.

Dan also said goodbye to me and asked me to let him know about the funeral arrangements. It was so surreal. Why aren't we going to see him again? He comes by every three or four days.

Will she die on my birthday? I think she wants to wait until tomorrow or the next day as she has always said that she'd die on the 12th.

Driving out to meet a friend for my birthday lunch, I became so incredibly sad. I feel this urgency about being with Mom, almost like I should cancel my lunch and go back—but I keep the lunch date.

Scott would pick the kids up from school and bring them to Mom's. He is being so accommodating and wonderful.

November 10, 7:45 p.m.

My despair and loneliness are overwhelming, and I just want to talk with my sister who has been so unavailable the last two days due to classes about adopting that she is taking. We'll spend more time talking later tonight and tomorrow, but I just feel this urgency right now. No one else will fit the bill. Only her.

Mom was positively hot tonight. I read in the pamphlet "Gone from my sight" that fever is common as people near death. She is so weak she even complained that Scott's camera was too heavy to hold tonight.

Sharon explained what Dan had said regarding her increased heart rate, skin integrity and fever. Mom seemed very interested that these symptoms mean she's close to death. Dan also told Sharon that she just has to decide to let go of this world—that is up to her.

I have a strong feeling Mom's spirit came to visit me shortly after midnight. Thank God for her, and for me, that we made it through November 10.

Laura and husband Scott, Mom and Sharon in carriage ride the night of Mom's retirement party.

> **Guests**
>
> 8-23-06
>
> Dear Ones: What a blessing to be able to enjoy your beautiful lake home one more time!
>
> The weather was perfect, the friendship shared was warm and wonderful, & your dear cabin was the best possible place to relax and hang out.
>
> I wish you many years & many memories in this lovely place.
>
> Love to you all —
> Mimi (Mom)

Mom's handwritten farewell note found at the cabin.

Nico, Sharon, Mom, Laura and Scott at the Ordway Music Theatre following Mom's being honored on stage.

Mom at age 4.

July 1946

For Mimi

Angels
The whisper of the wind breathes across the moonlight
As angels come out to dance in the night
They guide love and dreams
While gliding on the moonbeams
As darkness turns into light

Written by Hannah Preves Helgeson, age 9, in honor of her Mimi, November 19, 2006

Sisters Sharon and Laura

Mom's cats Nigel and Oliver

Mom, Mariah, Laura and Hannah at the playground

Young Jeffrey Siegel at the piano

Faith and Mom playing dress up

The Preves String Quartet

(From Left: David Preves, Mom, Doug Overland, Vince Bastien)

Hannah and Mom baking a castle cake for Hannah's 6th birthday

Mom was always so gentle, so very, very gentle. She has done this death so gracefully. This is a lesson for all of us. She had an elegance and incredible determination behind it, always holding herself so strong and beautiful.

Last night at dinner Hannah said that she didn't know what she was going to do without Mimi, how she was going to go on living. I told her that she was going to go deep within herself and find an inner strength that she didn't know she had—that she was going to find out that she is stronger than she ever imagined. I have certainly discovered this strength within myself through this process.

Sharon told me last night that she felt Mom's heart. Mom drew Sharon's hand close to her chest and as it rested there, Sharon felt her heart beating incredibly rapidly and erratically. She said that it (the heart beat) was so close to the surface of Mom's skin and that it felt "reedy."

One thing that Mom always did was to greet each day with joy. It was her motto for living, and her way of moving through time and space in the most graceful way possible.

We read from the book "Diary After Death" yesterday. One passage made me feel more comfortable and understanding of Mom's early demise. It said something about people being hurried along in this lifetime because they are needed as teachers in the next lifetime. Their skills are ready. They have to be taken so that they can do the work they were meant to do in the next realm.

Mom asked Sharon yesterday if her mother and her dear friend Carolyn would be waiting for her on the other side. She feels sure that they will be, and is so looking forward to being with them—and that their presence will welcome and comfort her.

I cleaned up Mom's room and brought her a lavender aromatherapy candle. The room feels so much more peaceful without all those vases of flowers and millions of well-wishing cards. I also gave her a pretty basket to keep all of her tapes, CDs. DVDs, and books that she wants to listen to.

Her whole room feels better, like it is cleared up for the work she needs to do in order to die.

Hannah crawled into bed with her yesterday. They were doing the silliest things. I haven't seen Mom with this much energy for some time. Mom was showing Hannah her face exercises so that she won't get wrinkles. Mom actually did these exercises for many years. She didn't have many wrinkles, so it must have worked. They were also doing Qi Gong exercises with their hands. Mom is so so sweet with Hannah.

Chapter 16
Active Dying

November 12, 2006

Today's the day Mom said that she would go, though it doesn't look like it. She has, however, taken a dramatic turn for the worse (or maybe the better, depending on how you look at it).

Mom just told me that someone keeps touching her leg, but when she opens her eyes, no one is there. She says that this has happened on and off all day.

When Melissa, the hospice nurse, was here, Mom said, "Keep touching my feet, it helps me to stay awake." I just realized that Melissa wasn't touching her feet at all. Mom was feeling this presence touching her feet.

We have had an interesting last two days. Sharon has decided to take up residence at Mom's house so that she can be by Mom until the time comes for her to either die or go into coma.

I've been spending a lot more time here, much to the horror of my 6-year-old daughter Faith. Sharon reminded me that this time with Mom is so brief, and that I have the rest of my life to spend with Faith. As a mother, it is so hard to put these things into perspective.

Faith is with her dad and her sisters after all. She's spending time with people who love her. But she has this way of making me feel like she can't go on living without me—and I fall for this completely.

Mom finally agreed to have a catheter today. I'm not sure she will be willing to keep it in. She says that it is very uncomfortable and wants it out, but agreed to give it six hours to try to get used to it.

She is so tired that she falls asleep while eating. This does not seem very safe. Eating will get to be too much of a chore soon. She can barely swallow. Everything is so uncertain. It is hard to wait.

Sharon said that she was visited by Mom's deceased best friend, Carolyn, in the middle of last night. She said she felt her bedroom door open and Carolyn's presence was there.

Maybe Carolyn is the one who is putting her hand on Mom's leg.

Sharon and I went out to lunch and both got take-out dinner because I haven't been able to focus on cooking lately. I'm going to let the kids skip their homework this week. Just too much to do. We can't keep going on thinking and acting as if nothing is happening here. We are suffering an enormous emotional loss, and need to take time to embrace that.

The Active Dying Stage: Monday, November 13

Margaret, the home health care nurse we had hired to care for Mom and who was most hands-on with helping Mom die, called me at eight o'clock this morning, crying. It sounded like Mom had taken a turn into the active dying stage.

When I arrived at Mom's at nine, she was still semi-conscious. This is so much more peaceful than yesterday. She seems like she is resting and so at peace. I told her I loved her, and she was able to say that she loved me, too. She also said that when Scott stopped by with the girls, Scott told her he "loves" her. Notice the tense used in the word *loves*. Mom even corrected Sharon when she filled in for Mom and said "Scott said he 'Loved Mom.'" She said to Sharon, use the correct tense "loves not loved."

Mom seems to be breathing only once every eighteen seconds or so. It started with once every 10 seconds this morning when I arrived, but now it is slowing down. We were told to expect her to slow down to one or two breaths a minute.

Margaret said that Mom's lips were blue this morning. She brought the oxygen in and Mom's color returned to normal.

Mom indicated that she wanted to see her friend Laurel when she called this morning so Laurel stopped by. Her last words were said to Laurel. She told her she loved her.

November 14

Mom's still breathing. She has been in a coma now since yesterday morning. Amazingly, she actually seems a bit better than yesterday, responding to a request for a sip of water by opening her mouth ever so slightly.

This is so depressing. It is so hard to see her this way. I wish her body would just let go so that she could be released from the hell of it.

Sharon and I kind of went into hyper overdrive yesterday—planning the memorial service before Mom even dies. It took several hours for us to realize that maybe we were getting ahead of ourselves. We were insistent on having the service this coming Saturday (today is Tuesday), but now seems a little ridiculous…. Planning and making so many phone calls allowed us to avoid experiencing the depth of how sad this is. Mom has always been so vibrant and energetic. It is so hard to see her this way, and it makes me feel slightly nauseous.

I had a terrible nightmare last night—it was so gruesome, upsetting and disturbing—something about being framed for someone's murder. I had a great talk with my sister-in-law about it today, and she felt that it is my psyche's way of working through part of this.

Mom is still breathing (10 p.m. Tuesday). While changing the sheets on Mom's bed, Margaret, who has a heavy accent from Africa, said, "Flip the pillow." I flipped it this way and she said, "No, flip the pillow." So, I flipped it the other way. And Margaret said "No." She grabbed the pillow and started to fluff it. I said, "Oh, you mean fluff the pillow," and broke out in a fit of laughter. We're still having humor despite all of this sadness.

My sister-in-law stopped by last night and brought us all coffee and chocolate. What a treat! She is such a strong and comforting presence. Today she took me out to a belated birthday lunch.

November 14

On Tuesday night at midnight Mom's body seemed to take a turn for the worse. All of a sudden she stopped breathing, her heart stopped and she started turning blue. Watching this was gut wrenching. Margaret, Sharon and I surrounded her bed to watch her pulse in her neck. The vein was bulging, beating heavily and fast. It would suddenly freeze, then relax and remain still. Then slowly, it would start beating again.

This happened many times over the course of the next few hours. Each time, we thought her heart would just stop.

Listening to her gurgling breathing sounds, I felt like I was watching someone be tortured. It was certainly torture for me to sit by and wait. At times I'd have to get up and go down to the living room to lay down on the couch—this our third night without any sleep.

When I lay down on the couch, I could still hear the terrible sound of Mom breathing. It was horrifying and I still have flashbacks. The only possible saving grace was that Mom was not conscious.

To pass the time, Margaret taught us African dance in the living room at 3 a.m. Still, we are finding joy among the sadness.

Chapter 17
Mom's Death

November 16

Mom died at 3:40 p.m. yesterday. What a tremendous labor she and we went through in order to usher in death. It was 56 hours from the time she went into a semi-coma on Monday morning until her death yesterday. The entire time was spent in this labor of horrific breathing. It started on Monday with what is called Cheyne-Stokes breathing. She would take in a breath, let it go, and then everything would stop for 10 to 30 seconds. It was eerie, and very hard work.

That breathing went on all day Monday and into Tuesday. We thought for sure she couldn't go on like this. Margaret kept saying, "She is a good fighter." I wanted her to stop fighting to stay alive and surrender to her death. What became abundantly clear is that I didn't have any control over this, and that acceptance was my best bet. This acceptance was incredibly difficult for me.

At midnight on Tuesday, her breathing changed. It went from the Cheyne-Stokes sound to a more labored shallow breath with a percolating or gurgling sound between each breath. I suppose this was the sound of her lungs filling with fluid. I could see her heart racing at her throat. It was an unbelievable sight.

By 4:30 a.m. I totally lost my ability to cope with the situation. It looked to me like Mom was being tortured. I was being tortured in the process of watching her terribly labored breathing, accompanied by a haunting, moaning sound. I couldn't get away from this sound anywhere in her small town home. I had to leave. I went home to rest and cry and get away from it for a while.

Scott held me in his arms when I arrived home in the early morning hours. I sobbed and sobbed. When I finally did fall asleep, I kept awaking, listening to his breathing, thinking how similar it sounded to Mom's labored death breathing.

Sharon asked me if I wanted her to call if things changed. I told her I wanted to be called only if Mom had actually died. I just didn't think I could handle watching and listening to the torture anymore.

After getting a few hours of rest and getting the kids off to school (what a godsend school is), I went back over to Mom's. There she was, still breathing away and moaning, looking bluer and grayer than ever.

We all decided to leave at about noon. My sister and I went out to the grocery store and to grab lunch. Margaret walked around the neighborhood. We did this to give Mom the space she possibly needed in order to give in to the death process. Obviously we were feeling desperate by this time. Leaving the house all at one time seems pretty much like grasping at straws. We were willing to do anything. Except, of course, the most obvious things give Mom the lethal dose of morphine.

Sharon and Mom had talked on three different occasions about the possibility of doing just that. Mom wouldn't hear of it. Sharon told Mom that in the hospice comfort pack in the refrigerator, there is a lethal dose of morphine at her fingertips. Mom wouldn't do that and said quite frankly "Yuck."

We followed her wishes. She didn't want an overdose and we didn't give it to her. Instead, we watched her suffer for 56 hours. During the first 24-30 of those hours she could still swallow.

At about 1 p.m. on the 15th, Mom had secretions come out of her nose and mouth. I was down in the kitchen. I heard this moaning cry come out of my sister's body. I knew something had changed. I went upstairs and Mom was completely blue. I thought that would be it. How could someone survive being blue, not having anything to drink for three days and drowning in their own secretions?

Margaret started checking her blood pressure regularly as it was dropping rapidly. After about half an hour, she did not have a detectable blood pressure. We thought for sure she would go within a few minutes.

Our sister-in-law Lonnie called and said she was on her way over. I called Scott. Everyone came over.

When Lonnie arrived it was about 3 p.m. Mom had been without a blood pressure for an hour or so—still laboring and laboring. I just wanted her to go, to give up the struggle. This was so hard to accept.

I sat in the living room with Scott deciding about picking up the kids from school in a half hour. Sharon's husband went into the bedroom and miraculously got her to leave the room, go downstairs and get some rest.

At this point it seemed our nightmare would never end.

Lonnie went up into the room with Mom and Margaret. When I went up to check on them, everything seemed different, like there was a sudden calm. The sheet was pulled up over Mom in a way I hadn't seen before. I thought she had died and asked what happened. They had decided to turn Mom over in what Lonnie called the "surrendering position." What a relief. Mom seemed so much less labored—like she had truly surrendered to the struggle. She was turned over on her right side—almost over onto her stomach. She was still breathing, shallow, tiny breaths. Lonnie had her hands on Mom's back and was holding and massaging Mom's sacrum. She asked me to come over and hold Mom's back firmly, more firmly than I ever would have expected to do with her very fragile and broken body.

Within just a few minutes it seemed as if Mom was taking her last breaths. They became slightly more shallow and then just stopped. I cannot describe the relief I felt when the next breath did not come. We held her back firmly for at least ten minutes. It seemed that if we let go, she might start breathing again, and holding her back firmly was our way of showing her to death's door—and ushering her through it.

**Caring Bridge Entry:
WEDNESDAY, NOVEMBER 15, 2006 07:32 PM, CST**

Hello Dear Friends,

Our sweet mama made her transition peacefully this afternoon surrounded by loving family.

Thank you for all of your kindness and dedicated support.

We will update this site soon as we finalize arrangements for Mom's memorial service.

We are now taking private time as a family and look forward to receiving your loving care via Caring Bridge.

In lieu of flowers, please send memorials to the Saint Paul Chamber Orchestra.

Our love to you,
Sharon and Laura

Following Mom's death, Margaret called the hospice and her agency to notify them. We were so thankful to have Margaret as our health care nurse. Now we just had to wait for our nurse Dan to come examine Mom, call the cremation society and for them to take Mom's body away.

Chapter 18
A Visit from Mom

November 18, 5 a.m.

I've been thinking about what a narrow window Mom had to pass through in order to be released from her body. It seemed like the size of a pinhole, so small, yet so important.

All of the books tell you to let your loved one know that it is all right for them to go—that you will be okay without them. I think Sharon and I did this too much. On Saturday, November 11, before my birthday dinner, I told Mom that it was okay if she left during our dinner. She took my hand, looked me in the face, and said, "Shhhhh."

I talked with my sister about this the next day. She said that Mom had said on Sunday, that we didn't need to say that anymore, that she knew it was okay with us. I have this weird guilty feeling now that she thought we were trying to kick her out of this world, her body, our lives. Rationally, I know that she didn't think this, but there is some part of me that feels she thought we were trying to get rid of her.

At the end I was so relieved when she finally left her body. She suffered so enormously for the last three or four days. I felt it was like watching someone be tortured by their body. After she took her last breath, I felt for the first time in weeks that I could actually take a deep breath. I think anxiety had made it difficult to breathe.

November 19, 4:30 a.m.

It seems like I can never sleep at this time. I'm always up trying to get myself to breathe. I feel panicked over all of the details of the memorial service, and over having to do Thanksgiving this week. Logically, I know that all of these details don't matter. I'm just having a hard time with my mind racing.

I feel like I need a little time to just fall apart. I can't afford to let myself do that right now. It just seems like there is too much to do. I'm in this perpetual motion state. Ickkk!!!!!!

November 21

We are now completing the plans for Mom's memorial service. I think it's going to be a really lovely day.

I woke up to the greatest e-mail today. Mom's friend, Carol, wrote to say that she could watch the kids in early December while Scott and I get away for a couple of days!!! I can't believe the upbeat feeling I have. The idea of a couple of days of respite is incredibly exciting, like there is a light after all of this hard work. I realize we've been living in this perpetual nightmare since August 1.

Finally last night as I was falling asleep, I felt like I could let my guard down while I was sleeping and not worry that someone was going to call me and tell me that Mom had died. I didn't realize I was so tense as I fell to sleep each night.

I'm meeting Sharon for lunch at our old hangout that we often went to with Mom. It seems kind of nostalgic to be here. I have never been a nostalgic person, but I'm finding myself wanting to wear Mom's jewelry, clothes, and go to places she used to go.

I can't believe she's not here any more. She was so young. It doesn't make any sense.

November 22 5:30 am

I just had the most unbelievable experience. The energy that is Mom entered my bedroom. I first noticed a tingling feeling. Then I saw that the rod used to turn the mini-blinds was parallel to the floor. I felt this incredible energy moving toward me, like a ball of light. I could see leaves through it, almost like you'd see through blinds when the moonlight is shining. My skin was electric. The whole room was electric. My ears were ringing. All I could do was reach out my arm toward the light energy and repeat over and over, "I love you Mommy."

Chapter 19
Memorial Service

November 26, 2006

The memorial service on Saturday was an incredibly beautiful event. Just as we suspected, about 500 people attended. I can't imagine how many there would have been if it weren't on Thanksgiving weekend.

Mom, Sharon, and I had planned the whole thing. I find it hard to describe just how beautifully moving the service was. The music—Catherine Wilson with her raw, heartfelt voice belting out "El Shaddai" and "Wind Beneath My Wings." Mom wanted that one to be dedicated to Sharon and me.

Larry David playing the piano so delicately and beautifully. The string quartet from the chamber orchestra that played Dvorak was visibly moved while they played.

My sister spoke so beautifully about Mom, telling stories of her youth and the special things she and Mom shared like the "Good morning to you" song, and when Mom taught her to always find at least three good things from a bad situation.

I spoke as well. I only hope my words were as inspiring and meaningful as Sharon's.

My Tribute to Mom
(by Sharon Preves, delivered November 25, 2006)

Good morning. Thank you for being here. It feels wonderful to be in a room filled with and surrounded by people who love my mom so much.

You each know or were touched by Alice in your own unique way. I have the honor and privilege of sharing with you today what it was like to be Alice's daughter.

I always knew I was loved. My mom believed in me and taught me that I could do anything I wanted to. She infused our home with music and song. When I was a child, Mom would come into my room in the morning, raise the shades and break into a rousing rendition of "Good Morning to You!"—a song which I actually must sing for you now so that you can truly appreciate and imagine waking up to Alice singing this first thing in the morning:

Good morning to you!
Good morning to you!
We're all in our places, with bright shiny faces.
Good morning to you!
Good morning to you!

Good morning, good morning, the little one said.

And now let us say,
*Let's have a great da*y!

She sang this song to me even when I was a grumbling teenager sleeping until noon. Mom continued this tradition well into adulthood, singing in the mornings on our recent annual mother-daughters' trips we took with my sister. My husband, Nico, and I have adopted the "Good Morning" song into our own lives, greeting each other with this delightful tune in the mornings.

At bedtime, Mom and I would sing a call-and-response version of "You Are My Sunshine," replete with kisses and nose rubs as we traded the verses back and forth. I had the privilege of singing both of these songs to her frequently in the mornings and evenings during the last weeks and days of her life.

When I was nine years old, the day our family dog died, my mom taught me the "find three things" game. She told me that whenever something sad or disappointing happened, I should be sure to try and find at least three good things that were a direct result of that which was causing me sadness. This is a life lesson that I have carried with me since that time and use, even today, in helping me to change my perspective or perception when I need to. I can tell you that I have been able to find far more than "three things" I am grateful for as a result of my mother's illness and death.

One of the gifts Mom gave to our family is the openness and grace with which she faced her own mortality.

The celebration of Mom's life we are having today is a direct result of her handiwork and planning. Indeed, Mom started planning this and other "going-away parties" within minutes of being diagnosed with cancer in August. In that diagnosis meeting, Mom actually announced to her dear doctor, Laura, and me that she was going to officially retire from the St. Paul Chamber Orchestra because she didn't want to miss out on a good party. And what parties you threw for Mom! Not every daughter gets to celebrate her mother in such a grand and public fashion. Thank you for the wonderful memories and all of those standing ovations!

Mom delighted in planning her memorial service. She loved looking at pictures of the sanctuary and hearing what Laura and I planned to say at the service. She said it was going to be "quite a party" and "wow, that looks delicious" as we poured over the picture food catalogue provided by the caterer. She loved this space and she and I share precious memories of Shir Tikvah's high-holiday services here together.

Mom modeled for me that it was okay to laugh and cry together openly during her illness. One night in late August during intermission at a musical, she told me that she thought she wouldn't live too much longer. We stood together and held on to each other, wracked with sobs in the lobby of the theater, making quite a scene. While we cried together, she held my face in her hands and said, "Isn't this beautiful?" And she was right. Our openness in loving one another was always beautiful. It was then that Mom told me that when she died she would always be able to hear me, even if I couldn't hear her. That is comforting to me now and I do continue to talk to Mom.

Indeed, I feel that she is taking care of me even now, spiritually, by showing me what it is I need to grieve well.

Mom showed me how to live out loud. She kept a jar of jelly beans in her home that I have come to call the "jelly bean jar of happiness," which gave frequent sustenance to my family.

In the last week and a half of her life, Mom not only went to a musical ("The Full Monty"—or as she put it The Half Monty because she only made it to the first act) but engaged in her civic duty by voting as well. One day well into her cancer I asked how her outing with her dear friend Laurel was. I asked what it was they had done together and she responded by saying, "We were just out there in it." And that's how Mom lived her life; she was just "out there in it."

I'll share one final story with you this morning. Two years ago, Mom and Laura accompanied me to Hawaii while I was teaching there. Mom bought this beautiful ceramic bell when we went to Chinatown in Honolulu. Upon returning home Mom created a delightful morning ritual that involved the bell. Although she shared her home with no one other than her two cats, Nigel and Oliver, when she was ready to leave the house every morning, Mom would ring her bell and announce out loud, "Here I come world."

So, in honor of Mom, I will ring her bell for all of us to share in giving her a proper sendoff. "Here she comes world " RING THE BELL FOR MOM

I sure hope you can hear us, Mom I love you.

Sharon asked me to speak after "Wind Beneath My Wings" because she didn't think she'd be able to speak at that time. Apparently that song, and Catherine's heartfelt delivery of it, touched many, many people as the whole congregation was crying during the performance. As I sat huddled next to Hannah, big tears were rolling down her sweet cheeks. She was finally crying. Thank God for that.

Somehow, I pulled it together to get up on the pulpit and speak. Sharon and I had a deal that we'd go up and stand next to the other if either of us were having trouble with our composure during our talks. Amazingly, we both made it through. The strength within has constantly surprised me during this process. We all have untapped strength. We just didn't know it was there.

Memorial Speech
(by Davida Laura Preves delivered November 25, 2006)

Thank you kind friends for coming to this gathering honoring my dear, sweet Mom. Your support and well wishes over the past few months have been appreciated beyond what words can express. It became abundantly clear to me how well-loved my Mom was by so many. Through your Caring Bridge entries, cards, flowers, phone calls, visits, and prayers, it also became clear how many she has touched through her gentle, loving guidance in the form of teacher, coach, friend, colleague and certainly as mother and grandmother.

I have been so blessed to have Alice in my life for my entire 41 years. To be loved by her, taught by her, led by her example, listened to, and guided in the most gentle and caring way. Everyone should be as blessed as I have been. I am truly lucky to be standing here today saying that Alice was my mom—that she loved me dearly my whole life.

The other blessing that my entire family shares is that Mimi was the best grandmother ever, loving and guiding my children in the most careful and thoughtful way. Playing with them, nurturing them, loving them. She did this every day and every night. Mom was always a presence in our home, always bringing her gentleness to our household.

I truly believe that my husband, Scott, would say that Alice had the guidebook for mother's-in-law. She had the perfect way of being there, but not there, helpful but not meddling.

Through countless encounters over the last three months, I have consistently been told by others that my Mom was a light in their life. That she brought them joy, taught them how to live, and always displayed the grace and dignity and love we have come to know as Alice.

It is up to us all now to carry the message Alice has taught us well: To greet each day in joy. To be a blessing to our fellows. To walk the earth gently and with dignity and grace. I know that my Mom would challenge each and every one of us to do that. So, let's meet her challenge—and best it.

We have all been blessed by the incredible presence that was Alice. Take that blessing and spread it throughout your life.

More than anything, my Mom taught me one value that I try to live each day. Rather than trying to solve the problems of the world, tend your own garden. Nurture it, water it, and watch it grow.

Thank you and blessings to each and every one of you.

Even Hannah participated in the service. She used her gift for expressing herself through poetry when she wrote this poem in honor of Mimi just a few days after Mom's death. We printed the poem on the back of the program just underneath a picture of Mom when she was five. This image accompanied by words made an awesome impact.

Angels

The whisper of the wind breathes across the moonlight
As angels come out to dance in the night
They guide love and dreams
While gliding on the moonbeams
As darkness turns into light

Written by Hannah Preves Helgeson, age 9,
in honor of Mimi on November 19, 2006

Scott was so supportive during the reception. I had his full and undivided attention. He stood right next to me during the receiving line and supported me as I greeted the hundreds of friends who had come to pay their respects to our family. I found out once again that Mom made an unimaginable impact in the world—always positive, always, gentle, always with humility.

Chapter 20
Friends

November 27

You really do find out who your friends are through the loss of your Mom. Unfortunately, you also find out who your friends aren't. I have been so surprised and deeply hurt by a few people that I thought would be there for me without a doubt. I know it will take time to work through these feelings and decide if I still want these people close to me—when I know they won't show up for me in my most poignant moments.

On the other side, many people, mostly old friends, showed up in unexpected ways. One woman, Carol, a fairly new friend of Mom's, has been such a dear and supportive resource through this process. She was there supporting us as soon as we came home from the hospital from the stroke, and offered us incredible "thereness" throughout the ordeal. Most amazingly, Carol has offered to watch the kids next week so that Scott and I can escape for a few days up to Lutsen—the site of our family cabin and favorite get-away. I cried when she offered this. We weren't sure if we'd ever leave town again without the kids with Mom gone. Look at this, just one week after the memorial service and we're having a little escape!!

November 30

I have this deep sense of sadness and disappointment with humanity. I am so deeply saddened by the way my father, who was married to Mom for 28 years, and two of my friends have handled this process of Mom's death. They haven't shown up in any way, shape or form.

Sadly, I had expected both my father (who was estranged from both Sharon and me) and one of my friends to behave in this way. Why is it I still feel disappointed and shocked? Why do I keep expecting sane behavior from people who have shown that they are incapable of being there for me? What is wrong with me that I keep expecting something from people who don't have it to give?

The other friend (or former friend) truly has shocked me. I thought she was someone I could count on, rely upon, trust. Finding just the opposite has been such an enormous disappointment.

Kindness, generosity, integrity and wisdom need to inform my decisions and actions. Sometimes doing the right thing is incredibly difficult and oftentimes, it requires a great deal of humility.

I have to realize that when people behave badly, they have no other tools. If they had other tools, they'd either not behave so badly in the first place, or clean up their mess shortly after creating it. It is so sad that people hurt themselves and others by not having any skills to do it differently, better, with integrity.

The thing I keep on having to learn is that I am the one I need to rely upon—I am my own best friend, ally, confidant, advisor, mentor—that I can do this for myself. Grateful to know that, I will also admit that it feels incredibly lonely at times.

What a gift to myself to have learned I can depend on my own inner strength as my life goes on. This is something I want to instill in my children, and want them to know is available to them at all times.

December 4

Arriving at our Lutsen cabin about a half hour ago, I quickly checked the guest book as it is fun to see who has visited since we were last here. Our family owns this cabin but Lutsen Resort manages it as a rental, therefore we have a guestbook and love to read what our guests say.

After reading three or four entries, I turned the page and there was Mom's writing. The entry was dated August 23, 2006. Mom had come up here with Laurel to have one last get-away. I can't even describe the emotion that swept over me. I was filled with love, surprise, grief, despair, and gratitude. It seemed like one last good-bye from Mom.

What a sweet and wonderful surprise. I sobbed from missing her after I read her entry. I didn't think anyone, except perhaps Sharon, could understand the deep meaning of this guestbook entry.

Here is Mom's entry:

> *August 23, 2006*
> *Dear Ones: What a blessing to be able to enjoy your beautiful lake home one more time!*
>
> *The weather was perfect, the friendship shared was warm and wonderful and your dear cabin was the best possible place to relax and hang out.*
>
> *I wish you many years and many memories in this lovely place.*
>
> *Love to you all—*
> *Mimi (Mom)*

Chapter 21
A "First" Without Mom

December 3

I went over to Sharon's today to write thank you notes. When we saw each other after a week, we hugged. While we were hugging, it hit me with such strong emotion that this human being, my sister, was a part of Mom. And that by hugging her in some way I still was hugging Mom. She is my one true connection to Mom, and I am so grateful for her. I couldn't let go.

December 10: Hannah's Winter Choir Concert

This is the first time I've ever attended Hannah's Angelica Cantanti concert without Mom sitting by my side. I was surprised at how hard this was. All five choirs began to sing the first piece. It was beautiful. I started sobbing, the kind of crying that is so hard to control. Scott was off taking pictures and our oldest daughter Mariah was at home with the flu. It was just sweet Faith by my side, giving me lots of comfort.

Another God moment happened at the choir concert. Every seat seemed to be filled when we arrived at the church. There must have been 1,000 people there. Faith and I just started marching around looking for a place to sit. Every spot was taken. Something directed me right up front and on the side of the sanctuary. There, sitting next to two empty spaces, was my dear friend's husband who said that the seats were open—and in the second row!!!! He was saving space for the rest of his family who then sat down next to us. I felt so supported by these people as I grew up with this family and spent countless hours at her house watching movies and hanging out. I can only believe that God had stepped in and saved a place for us when there didn't seem to be any—and not only saving good seats, but next to dear friends.

December 12, 2006

I feel so wounded and broken. I'm holding it all together on the surface, but as soon as I skin my knees, everything comes out. What is hiding right under my skin comes rushing to the surface with the slightest outside injury—someone speaks to me crossly, I hurt my finger in the kitchen—it doesn't matter what it is, I just have this incredible woundedness that is waiting to scream to the surface, sneak out at any moment and cause me to sob and weep pitifully.

January 2, 2007

Here we are: 2007. I had such a hard time letting go of 2006, to see it end. I'm never going to see, touch, talk to or experience Mom in 2007.

Mom's home health nurse, Margaret called today to wish me Happy New Year. What a wonderful woman, and I can't imagine her job! Since Mom's death she's already helped another family through the death process. And she was present at the birth of a girl grandbaby. When asked how it was to be present at a birth instead of a death, she said "Birth, death... I've come to think of them as pretty much the same thing." What a wise woman she is, and having gone through this process with Mom, I can understand Margaret's viewpoint. Death is a birthing of sorts, most certainly it is a labor to make a transition from one realm to another.

Anyone who has the blessing of working with Margaret at the end of a loved-one's life is so incredibly fortunate.

Chapter 22
Probate Court

February 26, 2007

Today at the courthouse in downtown Minneapolis I was legally named as the personal representative of Mom's estate. I distinctly remember asking our lawyer to draw up a living will last August, when Mom was well enough to sign everything. He advised us toward probate instead. How did we ever end up in probate?

What a painful experience this is. So weird and otherworldly. Why is the court handling my mom's money? My sister and I are perfectly capable of doing this. I know this may sound simple-minded or just plain dumb, but I have an emotional block about what it is that we are doing in court. Mom had no debt!!!!!

May 2007

Probate again. I almost lost my temper with the lawyer today. He started probing me about why I cashed out some of Mom's money in order for my sister and I to pay our taxes (we ended up in a substantially different tax bracket for 2006 due to unforeseen financial matters that weren't handled as we focused on Mom). Why is this anyone's business but my sisters and mine? Why is this strange man yelling at me for using the money that Mom left to me?

Before hanging up, I told him if he had more questions, he would have to e-mail them. I knew that if I didn't get off that phone now, I would either yell at him—or cry. Thank God for my wisdom to know how to take care of myself and not hurt others.

Chapter 23
Selling Mom's House

May 6, 2007

Mom's house sold today. It was a miracle of sorts, selling during the first open house in a slow housing market. During the open house, my family was at a very special event at a church down the street. Hannah's dear poem "Angels," which she wrote to honor Mom at her death, had been set to music, and this was the world premiere of the piece also entitled "Angels." The piece was written for three-part children's choir, piano and solo viola. Mom's star student, Kirsten Doctor, flew in from Cleveland to perform. Hannah was also performing.

Trash Everywhere

Today is our city-wide garbage pick-up, and I am taking advantage of the service by clearing out a lot of Mom's stuff and leaving it on the curb for pick-up so we won't have to call a dumpster.

Overwhelmed with the process of cleaning things out, Scott took over for me and I went home to the kids. Scott got a little over zealous with his cleaning. When I went by Mom's later, there was garbage everywhere, and Mom's things were scattered all over the lawn: papers, boxes, tapes, music and receipts. The scavengers had come by and left a devastating mess, and I felt such incredible disrespect.

Crying and crying, I noticed some boxes that Scott had set out were not necessarily garbage. When I reached into one of the boxes, I found all sorts of recordings and music items mom had saved. And then my hand reached around something that shocked me into disbelief and great, despairing grief. Many years ago mom had her beautiful, long, graceful hand cast in plaster. Mom had this beautiful piece of artwork on display for many years. At one point it broke and I never saw it again—until that day outside with the curbside garbage. The plaster cast caught every minute detail of her exquisite left hand, and suddenly I grasped Mom's left index finger. Pulling it out of the box, I looked at each and every crease of my mom's beautiful finger. This moment was both scary and poignant—at the same time.

Finding this put me over the edge emotionally. I was sobbing uncontrollably when a neighbor stopped by to talk with me. I couldn't speak, being too distraught—it was like a piece of Mom was about to be thrown away forever.

Eventually I pulled myself together. I put the finger broken off the casting into my pocket and brought it home. What will I do with mom's finger?

Chapter 24
The Piano

June 15, 2007

Mom's piano arrives today. Much to my dismay, it needed over $12,000 of repair and restoration. I'm not a pianist, but I knew enough from the way it sounded in her studio to have a technician look at it before we had it moved. It is a "parlor" grand that was so much a part of my growing up. I remember when I was a teenager playing chamber music with that wonderful instrument—piano trios with my dad and Uncle Jeffrey. Piano trios are an ensemble for piano violin, and cello—I played the cello part on bassoon. My friend Tina, who played piano, and I would spend countless hours playing and singing Rogers and Hammerstein music. I still have that book, and I can't wait to sit at the keyboard and chicken-scratch my way through the music again. One of the most profound memories all these years later is that I fell asleep listening to my parents play chamber music in the living room. It seems in hindsight that this was a large part of my childhood—always chamber music. They were so dedicated to that lovely instrument.

In order to move the piano out of the studio, a large window in Mom's house had to be taken out. That was a wild, emotional experience as I watched the five strong men lift the instrument out of the window and onto the snow-covered ground. Right then, I felt like I was watching a major part of my life caught in the balance of that precarious situation. I hope today's move is easier.

I have had mixed feelings about spending so much money to restore the instrument. Was it a waste because no one here is at all expert at playing piano? Faith is studying, but she is an absolute beginner. Only time will tell.

As I anticipate the piano's arrival, I feel I did the right thing having it restored. I know it will be enormously comforting to me, like having a part of Mom right here in my home. When I had to decide three months ago, I felt I this was my only choice.

IT ARRIVED! What a beautiful sight and the sound is magnificent—so resonant. I have missed music so much. It seems like it is in my cells. I just feel more alive when I'm creating music.

Having spent the past two months readying Mom's house for sale, I wasn't particularly pleased it sold in one day. Why was I counting on still having it for a while? Maybe so the kids could use the pool like they did with their dad many nights after dinner. This was a wonderful chance for some alone time for me—and for him to bond with the girls.

In any case, we close on July 5. Sharon and I have spent so much time going through each and every item in Mom's house. For a woman who lived a fairly simple life, I was surprised at all of the stuff she had. It seemed endless, and here we are, at the end. I have been taken aback emotionally by this project. It seems like Mom's life has taken over mine. Maybe that's not such a bad thing, since she lived such a beautiful life.

July 5, 2007

What a great, enormous relief to close on Mom's house today. Soon I will be released from the whole probate experience!!! This process of settling Mom's estate has taken over my entire life. I can't imagine what I'd do if I had to go to work in addition to raising three kids and settling this estate. I am so grateful for the quality of my life and wonderful support system.

August 2007

Hannah had surgery this week to have her tonsils and adenoids removed. This week I missed Mom more than in many months. I just needed her loving presence and willingness to help and listen. I need help so much and there is no one to turn to. I need someone to step in and take over the caring for Hannah. She is so sick—throwing up and unable to swallow. Scott has been great—but he is not "my Mommy."

Wanting someone to make it better from the outside, and missing my Mom and her special ways, makes me feel so desperate. When I feel that way, I simply have to pull that help out of myself. What a great lesson I've learned—one I wish I knew decades ago.

Sending Hannah into the Operating Room:

These three angelic figures popped into the pre-op room just before whisking Hannah off to surgery. What incredibly lovely women—angels to say the least, with their beaming smiles and loving attitudes—these nurses who would assist with the surgery!

When they shuttled Hannah away in her big chair, I felt so helpless letting her go into such a scary situation without me there. She was clutching Teddy in her arms. Teddy was the bear that Mom bought for Hannah at a garage sale so that she could bring something to "teddy bear day" at school. Teddy has been her special lovey ever since.

I felt Mom's presence as Hannah was rolled down the corridor towards surgery. I asked her to go into the operating room and be with Hannah and the surgeons. It was so reassuring to know that Hannah had the loving care of her beloved Mimi in the room with her.

Chapter 25
One Year Post Diagnosis

July 31, 2007

A year ago today I was down at Mayo with Mom when we found out that she needed one more test to be sure that she truly had what looked to be a very aggressive form of liver cancer. I remember how detached, calm and surreal I felt about the news we were getting. Now, one year later. I've survived what in some ways has been the best year of my life. I've gotten to know my sister in ways I'd only dreamed about in my entire life before this. My husband and I are a team of immeasurable strength. And, most importantly, I've found an inner strength I didn't know I possessed.

August 1, 2007

Today is the day—one year ago—that we found out mom was going to die quickly. It felt so definitive—no chance for any treatment. In a way, that made everything simpler. We didn't have to go through the rollercoaster of hope.

My level of reflection and internal processing is going to take on a whole new life now, and I started marking time very deliberately exactly one year ago.

Yesterday I saw an ad for an art festival I attended last September. I remember very clearly how Mom wanted to join us but was too exhausted. I know that flashbacks from last year, and what has happen up to the first anniversary, will be an emotional journey, but I know I can manage them. At times I'll hurt, and other times things will make me smile.

That saying "whatever doesn't kill you will make you stronger" is so true!

I keep thinking about Tammy Faye. Her larger-than-life eyelashes standing out from that cancer-stricken face. I marvel at how she summoned the energy to do an interview with Larry King the day before her death. What Herculean effort that must have taken.

Passing through to the next world is such a mystery. It is also such an incredible gift to assist someone in doing so.

October 10, 2007

Mom appears to me....

Mom "came to me" last night, the room filling with a buzzing energy. My skin was alive with energy, and I felt some sort of touch on my legs. Was Mom touching me so I would be healed of this terrible head cold? The experience started with a dream. I was picking up our dear friends' children from their home and bringing them to the bus stop. I quickly transitioned from that dream to a semi-awake state of seeing Mom sitting on a bench outside a concert hall. She was wearing a very casual green outfit, something she wore a million times—not the fancy concert attire she would often wear at the performance hall.

The state I was in felt like complete hyper-awareness—more alert and acutely awake than ever, but unable to move my body. Mom did not speak. She merely smiled, or I should say beamed. She was quickly joined by my deceased mother-in-law, Arlene, who was in a more solid form—more matter-like. She was very chatty and the first thing she said was, "It is a very clear day today." It was obvious to me that this was a remark about the clearness of the channel between worlds, and not a comment on the weather.

Mom sat beside her in her semi-transparent state and just smiled. I asked Mom about whether our family should move from this house to another to escape neighbor problems. She simply responded with a wave of her hand as if to excuse the issue as being unimportant. I asked what she thinks about Hannah playing the cello. She stood up and simply beamed this enormous smile. I asked her to be with all the girls, because they need her so. I got the distinct impression that she would do so. I also got this same impression from Arlene. I asked Mom what she thinks of me studying to become an interfaith minister, and again, she simply beamed.

Arlene, being the spokesperson, indicated that she and Mom come together at times to watch over us, especially the kids.

At this point, I was overwhelmed with the intensity of the energy I was experiencing. Tears flowed down my face, as Mom was such a being of love. I wanted to wipe the tears, but couldn't move. I told Mom that I couldn't go on, that the experience was becoming too intense. At that point, I felt her energy withdraw, and I gradually came out of my paralysis. My skin still felt electrified and the room still buzzed, with the energy still alive all around me.

Finally able to move, I turned to Scott. I was in tears from such a moving and overwhelming experience that was so positive in so many ways, but sort of a little scary in its bigness.

Chapter 26
Remembrance Ceremony

October 17, 2007

Mom's one-year death date is fast approaching. What should I do to honor her and myself on that day? Surprisingly, Sharon doesn't know if she wants to participate. We have both discovered how incredibly different we are through this process of Mom's death and the year after. She is so sentimental and objects mean so much to her. I am not. I am so emotional, and connecting and expressing myself mean so much to me.

I have decided to invite five of Mom's dearest friends to my home for a small gathering. 1) Gloria, a musical friend for 45 years. Mom and Dad used to play chamber music at Gloria's home. 2) Ann:, another long-term friend who was very dear to Mom's heart. 3) Laurel, probably Mom's longest friendship, a dear woman with incredible fortitude and insight. 4) Carol, a recent friend of Mom's who she connected with deeply in the last years and days of her life, and 5) Janet, Hannah's dear Godmother.

What will that evening be like? Definitely something with candles and maybe a prayer—and hopefully lots of stories and laughter. Mom had a tradition of lighting the Yahrzeit candle (Yahrzeit means "year's time" in Yiddish) to mark the anniversary of her own parents' death. I'll never forget the presence the Yahrzeit light took up in our home during these dates—so incredibly significant and meaningful. Now I understand the significance of this tradition as I am now faced with upholding the tradition because of her death.

I'm also tossing around the idea of music. It seems that nothing is good enough to honor this occasion, and having someone outside this intimate circle come in to perform is not what I want.

The journey of the past year has been unexpected, painful, joyous, deeply lonely, hopeful, anger producing, sad, and deeply spiritual. I have received an incredible gift from Mom's death and the loss of the dear friendship of two people: The gift of knowing that I am enough. I have what it is that I need. I am there for myself. I am complete. What an amazing thing to discover. I am so blessed.

My Birthday: November 10, 2007

I was dreading my birthday this year. All I can remember is what was happening last year at this time. My brother-in-law is getting married today! What a great opportunity to make new memories.

November 15, 2007

This is the one-year anniversary of Mom's death. I hosted a remembrance gathering at our home. We made an altar filled with flowers, the Yahrzeit candle and a beautiful white candle to represent Mom's spirit. We shared stories about mom. Sharon joined us and she even brought a radio interview that allowed us to hear Mom's beautiful voice. Mom's dear friend Ann played a Chopin Nocturn on the piano that had been Mom's for so many years. What an incredible treat to hear that divine instrument played so well in my own home!

Here is the closing prayer of the remembrance ceremony:

I want to acknowledge the difficulty and the learning that has occurred this past year—the milestones that we've met with strength, angst, heartache, love, courage, and a brave face. We've managed to go through this first year with great dignity and perseverance. For me, Mother's Day was particularly hard. We have now accomplished all of these firsts. This, the first annual death day is the last among the firsts. Never again will we only have the memories of the first time we had a birthday without Mom, the first time we observed the high holidays without Mom, or the first Thanksgiving without Mom. We will now be filled with new memories, like the ones we're making right now. New memories to be cherished and celebrated alongside those more distant memories that are so sweet, dear and sometimes painful.

So, let us go forward into this coming year and know that Mom's gentle love is with each of us. Let us move through this year with more confidence, love and light. Let us now let go of the pain of losing Alice and move into this new year with renewed vigor and delight—expressing the Joy within each and everyone of us. Amen.

Our entire family has now experienced the "first" of many things—first Mother's Day, first Thanksgiving, first birthday—without our Mom and grandmother with us. However, I realized that before those "firsts," came the poignant "lasts." Once we knew our mother had a terminal diagnosis, we honored and celebrated the many "lasts." Last birthday call, last holiday, last time we read to her. Most importantly though were these "lasts." Last time to see her smile, last chance to hug each other, last "I love you," and being loved by the most wonderful Mother any girl could have.

So we go on, in love with our mother's memory, and with knowing how much she loved us, and wanted us to be happy. Grief is a funny thing—it shows itself when and where you least expect it, but I work hard to turn those moments into tiny yet meaningful and positive memories of someone special who is hard not think of every day. And for that, Mom, I thank you.

Afterword

Mom's death has been pivotal in my adult life. Ten months after her death I began studies to become an ordained Interfaith Minister. Two years after her death I began to play Native American flute—once again using the music ability and knowledge I had developed over a lifetime. I now use the Native American flute in my work as a minister to create an atmosphere of meditative peace and love. I feel certain that I have Mom's assistance and presence in my life at all times. I am comforted and deeply moved by this amazing relationship we continue to have.

Manufactured By: RR Donnelley
Momence, IL USA
June , 2010